GATEWAY TO PARADISE

GATEWAY TO PARADISE

Basil the Great

Edited by
Oliver Davies

Translations by
Tim Witherow

with an introduction by
A.M. Allchin

New City
London   Dublin   Edinburgh

First published in Great Britain 1991
by
New City
57 Twyford Avenue, London W3 9PZ
© 1991 New City

All translations by Tim Witherow,
with the exception of On the Holy Spirit, *which is by Oliver Davies*

Cover design by Duncan Harper

British Library Cataloguing in Publication Data

Basil, *Saint 330-379*
Gateway to Paradise
1. Christianity. Religious life
I. Title II. Davies, Oliver
248.4

ISBN 0-904287-37-8

Typeset in Great Britain
by
Chippendale Type Ltd, Otley, West Yorkshire
Printed and bound in Great Britain
by
Billing and Sons Ltd, Worcester

Series Preface

*We have been long familiar with the achievement of the Fathers
of the Church in terms of Christian theology and doctrine, and
no one can make a serious study of the Christian faith without
reading the great texts of the patristic age and following their
far-reaching debates. But it is not this aspect of the Fathers'
achievement which this series aims to explore. Rather, our
wish is to rediscover something of the personal conviction and
the deep spiritual vision which is luminously present in a
considerable number of patristic works, which have for too long
been neglected in favour of other writings which are of historical
and theological importance. But, according to the good patristic
maxim, the best theology is written by those who most deeply
conform their lives to God.*

*Any of the Church Fathers would be baffled by the explosion
of spiritual writing that we find in the modern age; the term
'spirituality' itself is a relatively recent invention. Their world
was one in which theology, the faith as expressed in the creeds
and spiritual experience formed a single unity in which each
element was dependent on the others. The same, alas, cannot
be said of us, and the surge of interest in spirituality must
be seen as being, in part, an attempt to reclaim this original
unity for ourselves.*

*There is much in the spiritual writings of the Fathers which
is timeless. Indeed, it is astonishing how fresh and topical
much of what they wrote can seem today, despite the gulf that
exists between their world of late antiquity and our own world
of advancing technology and mass communication. Perhaps*

it is human nature itself which is timeless, though there are in addition subtle points of contact between the emergent Christianity of the ancient world and our own age in which the Churches must discover their own roots in order to weather the onslaughts of secularism.

The Spirituality of the Fathers *will contain carefully chosen selections from the often lesser known spiritual writings of the Fathers, newly rendered into a modern idiom, in order to set before the public the great spiritual treasures of patristic literature. It is our hope that this will strengthen the Christian life of the Spirit in our own times, and that we may come to share in that living faith more fully, which the Fathers, in their own age, always defended and fostered, by their work and their prayer.*

Contents

Introduction

St Basil the Great is one of the outstanding saints and teachers of the Eastern Church. It is characteristic of him that people have always tended to think of him in company with others; sometimes in company with the other members of his remarkable family, most notably his sister St Macrina and his brother St Gregory of Nyssa; in company with the little group of theologians and ،ninkers, the Cappadocian Fathers who did so much to establish a true understanding of the Church's faith during the controversies of the fourth century.

For though Basil was a man who greatly appreciated the value of solitude and silence, he was above all a man concerned to build up true conformity to the Church. We can see signs of this in these pages in his desire, his ability, to promote unity and understanding between divided Christians. We also see it in his fatherly concern to strengthen the common life of the newly formed monastic communities of his time. He lived in an age when new forms of Christian living were springing to life. Some were so keen to emphasize the relationship of each individual with God that they neglected the importance of our inter-personal relationships. Basil is concerned to stress our need for one another and to point out the ways in which we can build up one another in faith and life. In the course of time he has come to be revered in the Eastern Churches as a monastic teacher almost as St Benedict has been in the West.

There are two vital points in Basil's teaching as a theologian which emerge clearly in this anthology. The first is his insistence that the mystery of God always goes beyond our understanding of it and our powers of definition. We need to use words to speak about God, but we need to recognize their limitations. 'Nobody is so blind and so stupid as to believe that they can reach perfect understanding; indeed the deeper their understanding, the more they are conscious of their ignorance.' The second is his teaching about the action of the Holy Spirit. Here Basil is a pioneer, one of the first theologians to write a treatise on the Holy Spirit. He loves to point out that while the Spirit is one, his actions are infinitely diverse. God adapts his giving of himself to the needs of each of his creatures.

This thought of a unity in diversity seems to lie at the back of much of Basil's teaching. He sees it as the key to true community in the Church and in the world. Though his words can sometimes be very demanding, he inherited the classical Greek love for balance and moderation. So he points to the need for an alternation of manual work, prayer and study in the life of the monk. We need to find a good rhythm. So he tells us we are not to treat our body so badly as to make it weak, nor to indulge it so as to make it obese. His advice can be very simple and down to earth. In a discussion it is wise to wait a bit before jumping in, and don't shout at the top of your voice so as to annoy everyone else, but speak loudly enough for people to hear you! There is proper proportion to be observed in all things.

Like the ancient Greeks too, Basil was very conscious of the beauty of the world, in all its variety and exuberance. But seeing it in the light of the cross, he could not but be aware of its transience, and the imperfection of what is finest in our present experience of things. His writing sometimes becomes full of a painful longing for the beauty or glory of God himself. He points us beyond this world to the great world which lasts for ever, the world of God's eternal kingdom.

It is here that we begin to see all the importance of prayer in his version of things. In prayer, time and eternity come together; in prayer, we learn to see the sorrows and afflictions of our life, as well as its joys and achievements, in a wholly new perspective. He speaks of the way in which the life of a community and the life of each Christian needs to be penetrated by prayer, so that in the end 'the whole of life should be a season of prayer.'

Basil lived at a time when many old institutions were collapsing, when a whole order of society was passing away. He had his part in building up a new order, a new society which sought to reflect the mind of Christ. That is one of the reasons why he can speak so directly to us today.

A.M. Allchin

Basil the Great: his life and works

Basil was born around the year 330 into one of the most illustrious Christian families of all time. His father, Basil, was the son of St Macrina the Elder, and his mother, Emmelia, was the daughter of a Christian martyr. Two of Basil's brothers also became bishops, and Gregory, Bishop of Nyssa, was to be one of the greatest mystical doctors of the Church.

Basil was educated at the rhetorical schools of his native Caesarea in Cappadocia, then in Constantinople and finally in Athens where he met and befriended the great orator Gregory of Nazianzus. He returned to Caesarea in around 356, where he briefly embarked on his career as a rhetorician until the need to devote himself more fully to God led him to receive baptism and to visit the major centres of the ascetical life.

As a result of what he saw there, Basil decided to withdraw into solitude not far from Neocaesarea, where he was later joined by other young men who sought the monastic life. It was here that he wrote the two *Rules* for which he is justly famous and which both laid the foundation for monastic life in the East down until the present day and had a considerable influence in the West. During this period Basil also founded a number of new communities. In 364, Eusebius persuaded him to become a priest and, in 370, he followed

Eusebius as metropolitan of Caesarea. As bishop, Basil was very active, founding many hospitals for the sick and hospices for travellers.

Basil was also greatly involved in the major controversy of the time, which divided the Church. This centred around the person of Arius and his teaching, known as 'Arianism', according to which the Son is not 'of the same substance as the Father' from eternity but is rather his first creation. Being supported in the East by the Emperor Valens, this heresy remained dominant, and Basil came under great pressure to submit to the Emperor and the Arian camp. Basil resisted however, and became the chief defender of the Catholic cause. His extensive and brilliant writings on the issue did much to ensure the defeat of the heresy and its eventual overthrow at the Council of Constantinople in 381.

When he died in 379, Basil left a substantial inheritance to the Church in terms of his theological, ascetical and liturgical achievement, which was to remain a vital force in centuries to come.

In the present anthology we have not concentrated so much on those works which tell us of Basil the theologian, although a number of fine passages from his important *On the Holy Spirit*, which establishes the divinity of the Holy Spirit, have been included. These reflect Basil's keen sense of the Spirit's capacity to transform us and to make us conform to the divine nature. But we have chosen for this anthology, rather, those texts which convey something of the spiritual and pastoral depth of Basil and his great skill with words. Extracts from the two *Rules* as well as *An Ascetic Discourse* and *A Discourse on Ascetic Discipline* show his great grasp of the truths of ascetical living, while the sermon *On Faith* is a fine example of his exploration of the meaning of faith. The treatise *On Paradise* holds out to us a wonderfully fresh and dynamic vision of heaven and the life to come (although the authenticity of this work has been questioned, it was long attributed to Basil and contains the rare combination of rhetorical skill and spiritual vision which is so typical of his writing). The treatise *Consolation in Adversity* is a fine study of how we can best come to terms with the suffering which is an inevitable part of our lives, while the extracts from his *Letters* show Basil's overriding concern with the unity of the Churches, whose division was for him the greatest scandal. They include also a number of moving and intimate instances in which Basil gives sensitive spiritual counsel to troubled souls, and which show that the brilliance of Basil the theologian was founded upon his living faith and the depths of his spiritual understanding.

Oliver Davies

Short Bibliography

Texts and Translations:

Clarke, W.K.L., *The Ascetic Works of Saint Basil*, London, 1925 (English translation).

Courtonne, Y., *Saint Basile. Lettres*, III vols., Paris, 1957–1966 (Greek text with French translation).

Deferrari, R., *Saint Basil. The Letters* (Loeb Classical Library), IV vols., London and Cambridge (Mass.), 1929–1939 (Greek text with English translation).

Jackson, B., *On the Holy Spirit and Letters*, The Nicene and Post-Nicene Fathers, Michigan, 1983 (repr.)

Migne, J.P., *Patrologiae cursus completus: Series graeca*, vols. 29–32, Paris, 1857 (Greek text with Latin translation).

Studies:

Bettenson, H., *The Later Christian Fathers*, Oxford, 1970, pp. 59–98.

Jurgens, W.A., *The Faith of the Fathers*, Vol. II, Minnesota, 1979, pp. 3–26.

Quasten, J., *Patrology*, Vol. III, Utrecht/Antwerp, 1960, pp. 204–236.

on paradise

The beauties of paradise

'And God planted paradise in Eden in the regions of the east and there he placed the human being he had formed'. Let us now think, my friends, about the nature of a paradise which could be worthy of God, a paradise which would reflect the style and taste of such a master craftsman . . .

It is written that God produced from the earth every kind of beautiful and entrancing variety of wood to delight the senses. And just as he wanted the human being he had formed to surpass all other forms of life, so he wished that the home of humanity should be equal to his skill. And so he produced a place surpassing everything else in his creation, whose eminence would not be overshadowed, a place of wonderful beauty and complete security, whose splendour shone brilliantly over everything, spreading a radiant light as the stars rose, and keeping the most pleasant balance of temperature the whole year round.

In this place where God planted paradise there are no violent winds, or extremes of seasonal weather. It is never troubled by hail or fiery whirlwinds or violent thunder storms or icy winters or wet springs. There are no sweltering summers nor dry autumns; but instead there is a constant peaceful balance throughout the year perfectly suited to the beauties of each, so that nobody need fear the onset of the next season.

And so the spring flowers are not destroyed by the premature arrival of the summer; nor are the summer and autumn fruit destroyed by blasts of scorching winds. But every season is assigned its proper place so that they proceed in an ordered round, calmly and without getting on top of each other or in each other's way.

And each season produces its own gifts as expected and without harm. The earth has a rich fertility sending forth streams of milk and honey, able to produce any variety of fruit, and surrounded by life-giving water. Indeed the water itself is immensely beautiful, both sweet and delicately transparent, providing great pleasure to the eyes and great benefit.

(1–2)

Nostalgia for paradise

First he formed the place itself which would be fit to receive all his creations, and then he planted there every variety of beautiful tree to caress and delight the human senses. How could I ever find a means to represent to your eyes the beauty of the home from which you were exiled, so that you would feel not just sadness and nostalgia for everything that you had lost but, by thinking back to that period before your exile, you could recall the beauty and pleasures there which were not yet mixed with pain and distress?

It is true that even here and now there are fields that are full of flowers, and that we can see beauty everywhere; however, true joy is revealed only to the mind. The rose conceals thorns, bringing pain with pleasure and showing us that all the pleasures of this world are mixed with pain. None of the pleasures we enjoy on earth is entirely pure, for they are immediately entwined with grief: marriage with widowhood, the raising of children with worry, birth with death, great honours with great disgrace, health with illness. The rose flowers, but it causes me grief. Each time I see it flower I remember our sin that caused the earth to put forth thorns and spines in protest. Thus its charm lasts for the briefest of periods and leaves us while we still long for it. For the moment we have plucked it, it begins to die in our hands.

But in paradise it does not blossom briefly and then wither, but retains its bloom throughout the year, never losing its flower. Its scent never fades nor does the gleam of its freshness disappear. The force of the winds and hurricanes does not harm it, nor do the periods of calm cause it to wither away. It is not frozen by the frost nor blasted by the heat of the sun; rather a gentle wind provides a light and pleasing breeze which preserves its bloom forever from the destructive actions of time.

(3–4)

Paradise contained the peak of perfection

The beauty of the plants reflected the work and planting of their Creator: the small branches bearing fruit, single-stemmed and many-stemmed, multi-leaved, darkleaved, deciduous and evergreen, those that bear fruit and those that do not, those grown for their usefulness and those for the pleasure they bring. All of them were exceptional in their size and beauty, dense with branches and thick with clusters of leaves and fruit providing an abundance of pleasure and benefit.

How could you find a way to represent the degree of pleasure there? If you compared it with anything in this world, your comparison would be absurdly inadequate to convey a true picture of the original. Everything there is perfect and fully completed. It did not grow gradually, slowly coming to maturity and then flowering in the course of time, but came into existence in an instant at the highest peak of perfection and power, not requiring human help.

(5–6)

Paradise the delight of humanity

In paradise there was every sort of bird, every type of feather and birdsong which would provide a wonderful and lavish spectacle for anyone to feast all their senses, sight, hearing, touch, smell and taste. And with the birds you could have seen and heard every possible animal species living at peace and in harmony with each other. And the snake was not an object of terror but was tame and harmless, and it did not creep along the ground on its belly but moved upright on its feet. For all those animals which are now wild and hostile were at that time tame and gentle.

It was into this environment that God placed the man whom he had formed. He formed him elsewhere and then introduced him. And in just the same manner that he had first produced the lights and then fixed them in the sky, he formed man out of clay and then placed him in paradise. You must note that what is written is not: 'Whom he had made', but: 'Whom he had formed'. For something that is made is done by following a model, but this was incorporeal and thus unconfined by place. So the process of making must necessarily come after the process of forming, as the soul must come after the body even though they must both exist together. Initially it is the body that exists but it is then followed by the soul that adheres to it and is made one with it since the body is not endowed with its own mental capacity.

But why have I tried to delight you by describing the pleasures of paradise and then to depress you by juxtaposing them with the life of pain? Surely because your mind, which is led beyond this world and sets out to its true home above, will understand and seek to attain all those things we have promised: 'Which the eye does not see, the ear does not hear, and the heart does not feel'. But who could know anything which the eye does not see or the ear does not hear? And if it does not strike a chord in our heart, how can it ever be accessible to our mind? We do not reject every bodily matter and desire everything spiritual. For as a rule everything we perceive with the senses also makes an impression on the intellect; and so while we can describe paradise in a physical way, we can also explain its spiritual sense through allegory. Thus in the sentence: 'And God placed Eden in the regions of the east', we are not told about everything which grew there, but we can know the exact location, which is delight: Eden must be interpreted as delight.

(7)

The pleasures of paradise are in harmony with the sacred

But what are these pleasures we have spoken of which enter the mouth, travel into the stomach and are eventually expelled and destroyed? Was this gift given to the human race by the grace of God that it should have a full stomach, a healthy body and an abundance of sensual pleasure? Was it this that could not be expressed in words? And should we therefore follow the path of excess and brutal arrogance, seeking to fatten our body and swamping our soul with physical excess in every possible sin?

We must realize that it is a very different idea of pleasure, and one worthy of God's creation which is meant. So what sort of pleasure could be in harmony with the sacred? Remember what is written: 'Show your delight in God and he will fulfill your heart's wishes'.

(8–9)

In paradise everything was full of the beauty of God

The varieties of virtue are infinite and its beauty inexpressible, because virtue comes from the complex intellect of God. Therefore it was written: 'God made paradise', not just in the east but: 'in the eastern regions'.

For everything that was planted by God shone with its own bright light of virtue. And flowing there we also find the river that delights the city of God and is the torrent of pleasure feeding and giving life to its flourishing spiritual beauty. This is the river named in the Bible which emerges from Eden and waters paradise. It is written in scripture that right at the very first moment of creation he introduced Adam to rule and be its master. But, on the other hand, he formed Adam and then created paradise. The reason is that the moment he had finished the home of humanity he introduced the master of it: so that he should not have to create a humanity that was poor and then afterwards have to produce riches to remove its poverty. So having created perfection from the outset, he then introduced people to it. For he knew the difference between the life existing outside and that which existed inside the confines of paradise, and by comparing them he realized both the excellence of the latter's beauty and the consequence of our fall.

(10)

God the divine gardener

In order to conceive of a garden that could be worthy of the hand and artistry of God, you should call to mind those words of our master to his disciples: 'You are the vines, my father is the gardener', meaning that they had been planted by him. For, from this planting, we begin to grow in the house of our Lord and bear fruit in the halls of our Lord, as is written. We find the same idea in the prophets: 'I have planted a vine which will be fruitful with perfect truth'. And remember those bold words that Paul said in imitation of Christ: 'We are the fellow workers of God, make yourself into his garden. I have done the planting, but Apollos will water it and God will ensure it grows'. And, 'The just man will flower like the vine'. David was likened to a tree planted beside a flowing river which: 'Bears its fruit at the appointed time and never loses its leaves', and similarly: 'You have brought the vine with you from Egypt and, having expelled the people, have planted it'. And so, guided by this evidence, you should be able to conceive of paradise in your mind and find yourself in the beams of divine light; from there you will find the source of divine light, and the site of delightful paradise. And if you can imagine a place on earth where the saints sit in the company of all those who have shone in the light of their virtue on earth, enjoying the grace of God and leading a life full of the pleasures of truth and happiness, then you would not be far from a reasonable image of paradise.

(11)

On being worthy of the pleasures of paradise

It is in that place of paradise that we can find the deep roots of all the virtues, which guided the saints, and on which humanity who emerged only recently must rely. And human beings must undergo a rigorous training if they are to overcome their great lack of virtues and reach the state of perfection.

And it is there that we can find the gathering of the saints, the origin of light and the soul's pleasure: and it was there that God placed the human race. If you consider this in physical terms, feeding your senses with delight, you can find an image of physical paradise full of the highest pleasure. But if you think of it in spiritual terms, leading your mind far above physical pleasures, and rising to consider the beauty of the angels, you can learn justice from their fruit, finding yourself reflected in the river of God whose surging waters delight the city of God which was made and constructed by God. And through this city flows the river that rises from Eden and waters paradise.

Consider all this and praise its maker who produced these benefits for your pleasure, and strive to make yourself worthy of this. And if you turn to him you will understand our origin and destiny because his is the glory for ever and ever. Amen.

(12)

Consolation in adversity

God allows pain for our good

J ust as a ship tossed by the waves of a storm will be dashed to pieces unless it has an experienced captain at the helm, so anyone who is in difficulties will find their spirit broken and their hope of salvation dashed unless they are guided by the teaching of the Lord. And so if any of you find yourselves in difficulties I suggest you listen to me as I offer you, to the best of my abilities, the consolation that comes from the scriptures.

Whatever your problems, you may be crippled and oppressed by poverty, or have lost your worldly position and been reduced to an ignominious life, disease may be sapping the strength of your body, you may have lost your children and friends, the troubles of the world may weigh down upon your mind and heart, your body and limbs may be covered with leprous sores, you may be shunned by the great majority of people – yet you must not allow yourself to be broken by such terrible afflictions but must seek inner peace in the teaching of God where you will find consolation for everything that oppresses you. If you can learn from the teaching of the Lord then, just as a good captain can steer his ship into the calm of the port, you will find yourself guided to the calm of inner peace.

You must not, my friends, think that it is out of hatred for us that God sends such punishments; rather it is in order that his love may be displayed through our just actions. The Lord himself, speaking through Solomon, says in Proverbs: 'My children, do not fall away from your adherence to the Lord because he has corrected you, for this correction is a sign that he loves you'. A parent will not hesitate to punish an erring child he or she loves most dearly, and a teacher will often strike a pupil in order to improve his or her behaviour.

(1)

The just benefit from suffering

The reason for God punishing us is two-fold: he punishes the just both to improve them for the future and to reprove them for their previous actions. I shall support this from the teaching of the Lord but, before I do so, I shall show that the just are punished so that, by these trials, their true worth can be revealed more clearly. As Jacob said in Canaan: 'My children, rejoice at the trials you encounter in the knowledge that these will reveal your patience and true faith'. And later on he said: 'Happy are they who are tested since, if they come through it, they shall receive the prize of life that God has offered to those who struggle on'. And so, my friends, we should rejoice when we suffer great physical pain or are tested by the harsh struggle before the Lord our judge.

It is not when everything is going well that we should rejoice in Christ but when everything is against us. Remember what Paul said: 'Let us rejoice in the hope of God's charity but not only then, but let us rejoice in the times of tribulation since they will reveal our patience, and our patience will show our true worth and our true worth our hope. Our hope will not come to nothing because the charity of God is poured into our hearts by the Holy Spirit which has been given us'.

Many great benefits have come to the just from their experience of suffering. And in the same way that the earth would not be fertile and rich unless the farmers worked hard to cultivate it, and without whose efforts it would not only cease to offer up its produce to the human race but would turn into its opposite and bear thistles, so if decent people were not relentlessly afflicted by adversity they would not only fail to progress but would repeatedly slip and fall from the right path. We have learned this from the teacher mentioned above. For there was a man who was conscious of his own virtues and who had come before the Lord secure in what he deserved. But having been taken to the third heaven and led into paradise, and hearing words which no one can speak, he discovered that divine providence had sent the angel Satan to scourge anyone so full of pride they forget to be grateful for what has been given to them. He was delighted at this and wrote to the Corinthians: 'I shall not extol the revelation from the heights since I have been given a goad for my flesh, the angel Satan, who will strike me if I am boastful. Three times I called out to God to stop him, but he answered that his grace should suffice for me; for virtue is perfected in weakness', and again: 'I rejoice in my weakness, my persecution, my distress for Christ for when I am weak then I am strong'.

(2)

The love of God extinguishes grief

And so let us be glad and bear with patience everything the world throws at us, secure in the knowledge that it is then that we are most in the mind of God. In this life you would have to be very naïve to expect that, after enjoying a lifetime of luxurious abundance, you could then receive the celestial gifts in the next life. Which of the saints was able to avoid and be free from the dangers of this world? If you examine their lives carefully, you will find that none of them managed to escape the tribulations of this world but, having endured all the trials of this world patiently, they arrived at the incorruptible glory of truth.

The patriarch Abraham had such a deep faith and love of God that he was prepared to sink his sword up to the hilt in the body of his dearest son. He chose to be regarded as a murderer rather than as unfaithful to the commands of God, prefiguring the words of our Saviour who said: 'If you love your son or daughter more than me you are not worthy of me'. And so to be seen as worthy of the Lord, he followed the divine command and offered his only son as a sacrifice, feeling no sorrow that he should be killing his own heir. Why should he not feel grief? The reason is that his heart was burning with the love of God and the heat of faith which extinguishes all grief. This was the sort of man the patriarch Abraham was, someone who truly loved God and about whom the Lord has spoken in witness: 'Now I know what you are since you fear your Lord and have not spared even your dearest son for me'. Even he could not live his life without such trials and tribulations but endured everything and deserved to be called the father of all the saints.

(3)

God, the heavenly doctor

Do not, my friends, feel pain at your physical afflictions, but be strong and thankful for whatever the Lord sends. If your body is racked with every sort of pain, do not become depressed, allowing your spirit to be broken, and do not feel driven to cry out against God; but instead you should call to mind the example of Job who surpassed all others by his patience. Remember what he said: 'As God chooses so it will be done, may his name be praised'.

I have known people whose bodies were covered with the marks of leprosy, and had reached such a peak of desperation because of this, that they were convinced that they had been utterly abandoned by God. Anyone who thinks like that does not understand the teaching of God. Each of us ought to concentrate night and day on the divine law so that we may realize that 'God is the real justice and justification himself, which is more valuable than gold and precious stones and which is sweeter than honey' and which provides the real cure for disease. For the pain of the disease will only last for a short time, while the spiritual healing will last for ever.

Believe me, my friend, the body can never be cleansed of dirt to the same degree as the soul can be purified. And does not the doctor who is to cure the sick person of disease sometimes make an incision in the skin with his knife or even, when necessary, use a flame to remove the pain which the disease has produced? Now you would never accuse a doctor of doing this out of hatred but would actually reward him with presents. God, the heavenly doctor, with his fatherly affections has a much greater desire to help those whom he will save from death. And for this reason he sends us temporary blows so that he may free our soul from the blows that produce everlasting death.

(8)

Cleansing the soul

And so, my friends, accept whatever the Lord sends with a willing spirit and do not groan at what is imposed on you, for why should you feel joy at being part of that crowd or pain at being excluded from it? Rather we should do everything to ensure that we are not excluded from the city of God. For those in the cities who seem so secure within the protection of their walls will discover that, if they are struck down by the sickness of corruption and neglect their real life, then they will be excluded from the heavenly city, which is the mother of all the saints. Even though you may feel pain and sorrow at being excluded from the cesspit of the city, you should tolerate it wisely, ensuring that you serve God with humility and prepare yourself for the citizenship of his city and paradise. For you have been excluded from contact with the masses not because of the state of your soul but by the nature of your illness; it is an illness which is what they call infectious. However it will not infect your soul but will serve to cleanse it.

And so I encourage you to put aside your distress, my friends, and your depression and not allow the pain to lead you to despair of the future. Do not believe those stupid people who think they will be reborn in their present bodily form on the day of resurrection, since this is merely a vain and baseless piece of superstition. Indeed I challenge anyone who believes that to show me the page of the Bible where it is written. I have certainly never seen it and I am sure that, if they had taken the trouble to study this matter carefully, they would not have committed such a lie and blunder.

But then ignorance produces a wretched soul, and a mind full of nothing does itself terrible damage! Still, my friends, let us leave this exposure of their ignorance of the Bible and find wisdom in the words of God. Let us look to God and say: 'Give me intelligence and teach me your words, happy are those whom you have taught, Master, and schooled in your laws so that they can find courage in times of need'. And so if the Lord has taught you the way, then you will never be tossed by the storm of lies around you.

(9)

Suffering, a prelude to the resurrection

Remember the hope that Job maintained even in the midst of his terrible sufferings, and the strength he showed when his body was racked by pain. For he believed that the pain was preparing his body for the day of resurrection. Listen to what he said: 'I know that my Redeemer lives, and on the appointed day I shall be resurrected, and once again I shall be made whole and in my flesh I shall see God whom I myself and no other shall see. It is this hope which I keep in my heart'. And you too, my friends, should have the same hope and trust that you will reach the splendour of immortality in the next world, for this hope will make your present pain seem light and easy to bear. Indeed, the pain will no longer seem to be a punishment and source of grief but will serve to fill your spirit with joy.

If we seem to have spoken rather too briefly about the transformation of the body, then we need only recall the words that Paul spoke with great clarity and at some length in answer to those who were uncertain or in doubt on this matter. They had asked him how the dead would be raised and in what physical form, and he replied: 'You fools, nothing you sow will have life unless it has first died. And what you sow is not what will become the body but just the seed, like a grain of wheat or something similar. It is God who gives body to each as he sees fit'. For a simple grain of wheat which is sown on the ground does not appear to possess any sign of life, and yet, once it has rotted into the ground, it thrusts up its head and produces numerous ears and a luxuriant clothing of vegetation around itself; this is what is meant when it is said that it is God who gives body to each as he sees fit. In the same way the corruptible body that has been buried deep in the ground has no life of its own unless, like the grain of wheat, it possesses the seed of life. And when, at God's command, the time of resurrection arrives it is not the corruptible and seeded part that shall be resurrected but the incorruptible and immortal part.

So it is written in a passage that comes later: 'What was sown in corruption will rise without corruption; what is sown in contempt will rise in glory, what is sown in weakness will rise in strength, what is sown in the body will rise as the spirit'. This means that the body we have at present will be destroyed immediately after death and will rot and feed the worms. Even before death it is continually disintegrating; even before the final breath has been breathed, the limbs of our body start to grow weak and begin the process of decomposition. It has to suffer abuse and countless infirmities, hunger, thirst, fatigue, tension, and extremes of temperature, for in this life we are composed of the physical and the spiritual. It is the spiritual part of us that will rise again and be formed anew by the Holy Spirit as it is written in the Psalms: 'Let your soul depart and they shall be created and you will renew the face of the earth'.

At present we have a human body but in the future we will have a celestial one, because there are human bodies and celestial bodies. There is a human splendour and a celestial splendour. The splendour that can be attained on earth is temporary and limited while that of heaven lasts forever, which will be shown when the corruptible becomes incorruptible and the mortal immortal.

Have no doubt, my friend, that you will have a celestial body and do not think that just because your present body is covered in leprous sores or any other blemishes that you will be excluded from the splendour of heaven for that reason. On the contrary, as the examples of Lazarus or Job remind us, you will be even more deserving to enter the kingdom of heaven. We will only be excluded from the kingdom if our faults and sins remain within us. And we shall be excluded from the kingdom if we think that our omnipotent Lord is powerless. The only person who could think that God is powerless is someone who believed they could not be improved by him. You surely do not believe that the Lord, who can reanimate and revive arid and reduced flesh and bones, would be incapable of transforming them into the splendour of heaven? You cannot agree that God is omnipotent and then claim that in this particular area he is completely powerless!

(12)

Suffering leads to spiritual growth

You may perhaps be led to despair of life, thinking that you have been abandoned by everyone and that you have been covered in sores because of the sins you have committed. But you ought to regard this as the sign of God's love rather than his hatred, because in this life God wishes to correct us, his children, so that our spirit may be received by him in a spotless and pristine condition. As it is written in the Bible: 'God rebukes those he loves and punishes each child he accepts'.

And so if you see anyone committing great sins and yet never being punished for them and whose body is never afflicted by illness or misfortune, you may be sure that they have been abandoned by God because of the magnitude of their sins. Such a person is not punished because they are not worth saving; while you are rebuked so that you are not consigned to eternal death. This is what David said: 'The Lord rebukes me so that I shall not be consigned to death'. And even Jerusalem, when it committed a crime against God by killing the prophets whom he had sent to redeem it, suffered destruction and captivity in Babylon so that, by these means, its children might be put back on the right path: a punishment intended to lead to correction. And so when the seventy years were over the city was restored to its former glory. God showed pity and offered these words of consolation through the priests in Jeremiah: 'We have spoken, my priests, to the very heart of Jerusalem and we have offered consolation: for it has drunk from the cup of divine anger and has received twice as much punishment from the Lord for its sins'.

If you are a good Christian, you should be pleased if you suffer troubles, since you will become more worthy. And if you are a sinner, you should be pleased if you are afflicted, for in this way you will be cleansed of your sins and will find consolation in the time to come. Affliction offers benefits in each case, for: 'The spirit which has suffered is a sacrifice for God; God does not despise the heart which is contrite and humble'.

If a sinner is rebuked by God but refuses to change their old ways, merely despairing for their life, and saying: 'I have no chance of being pardoned, God has abandoned me, my whole life is heading for disaster, I can expect no peace after I die. Such a person signs their own death warrant and falls on the sword of desperation, joining the group denounced by the prophet when he says: 'You have rebuked them and yet they show no remorse, you have punished them and yet they ignore the warning'.

But you should do everything, my friends, to avoid becoming one of that group, and be ready and willing to take to heart the judgement of God when he says: 'The judgements of God are sweeter than honey'. Even though the punishment may seem harsh at the time, it will produce a wonderful yield in the future. Such punishment will steer you away from sin and lead you to virtue. You will overcome death and find life because of it. You will avoid terrible punishment in the future and gain an eternity of joy. You will be led away from pride and towards the peace and humility of God.

Remember this: 'It is good that you have made me humble so that I may learn your justice'.

If you have taken what I have said to your heart and continue to remain true to his praises and his grace, continually giving thanks to God, you will always feel the spirit of God within you. For anyone who keeps their mind on God will never be without him. He will soothe the pains of your body and strengthen its capacity to endure; and even if your body is covered with festering wounds, you will be able to retain your mental composure and balance, with the help of our Lord Jesus Christ, who lives and reigns forever. Amen.

(13)

on Faith

God transcends our minds and our words

It is indeed a good thing to keep the thought of God uppermost in our mind and something that a true Christian should never cease doing. To express such thoughts in words, however, is a very different venture. For our intellect is far from being adequate to deal with this subject, and the language we have to express the thoughts of our intellect is weak and obscure. And since our intellect is so unequal to this task and our language is inferior to our intellect, then would it not be better to say nothing and avoid offending the majesty of this subject by the poverty of our language?

For while the desire to glorify God is naturally present in all rational beings, the ability to express such matters adequately is not equally present. Nobody is so blind or so stupid as to believe that they can reach perfect understanding; indeed, the deeper their understanding, the more they are conscious of their ignorance. Thus both Abraham and Moses, who reached the height of what human understanding can achieve, felt only their worthlessness in the face of God. Abraham said he was merely dust, and Moses thought his voice weak and his tongue slow. For he saw that his tongue was incapable of expressing the complexity of the intellect. But since my audience is here to listen to me speak about God, and the Church is always ready to listen, as it is written: 'There can be no end to listening', I feel I am entitled to speak to the best of my ability.

We will not speak of God as he is, but only as he is accessible to us. However, since we do not use the fact that we cannot possibly see everything between heaven and earth with our eyes as a reason for ignoring what we can see, then we can fulfil our duty with these few words, while being ready to concede that to deal with the whole subject is beyond our powers. For even if we had the tongues of angels or archangels in all their natural intelligence, we would not be able to deal with a mere fragment of the subject, let alone with all of it.

And so if you want to speak about or listen to God you should seek to transcend your body and its senses, rising far above the earth and the sea, and leaving the lower atmosphere behind you; travel beyond time and the earth's natural rhythms and orders; soar above the stars with their wonderful forms and sizes, and everything that gives them their harmony, light, position and motion as they are attracted and repelled from each other. And once you have gone beyond these, rising up through the sky and gaining height, look around with your mind at the beauty there, the celestial hosts, the choirs of angels and archangels, the glory of the dominions, the rows of thrones, the power, authority, and majesty. And then, having passed through all these, contemplating every one of them with your mind, you will finally arrive at the divine nature, which is still and motionless, changeless, passionless, simple, elemental, indivisible, inaccessible to light, of ineffable power and boundless size, of overpowering glory and inconceivable beauty, which exercises an irresistible attraction for the wounded soul, but which cannot be expressed in words.

The Godhead is Trinity

There you will find the Father, the Son and the Holy Spirit, whose nature was not created, whose power is sovereign, whose essence is goodness. You will find the origin of all, the cause of all that is and the root of all that lives. This is the source of life, wisdom and virtue, and the pure image of the unseen God, the Son born of the Father, the living Word, the God who is, and who is with God, existing from before all time and not acquired; the Son, not a possession; a maker not an artifact; a creator not created.

For everything that exists is of the Father and the Son. And everything that is of the Son is of the Father too, as the Lord has told us saying: 'Everything that the Father has is mine too'. Everything that is in the original is also in the image. For as scripture says: 'We have seen the glory of him, the glory of the Father's only Son', which means that such powers do not come to the image externally by some form of gift, but because of the natural communion which the Son has with the majesty of his divine Father. For he has not received some attribute in the usual fashion but rather possesses it by his nature as a consequence of his Father. And so as a Son he takes his nature from his Father, for as the only child he contains everything without division.

Thus we speak about the Son as being of the same nature, and not created by decree, whose being shines in its unbroken light, in timeless unity with the Father, equal in power and goodness in his majesty. For is he not a sort of image and seal displaying the Father in himself? Everything that comes after this, the dispensing of salvation to men and women and the revealing of his presence through the flesh, declares that the Son who has been sent is powerless by himself and accepts his mandate, so that there is no reason for you to diminish the divinity of the only Son. For you should be humble and recognize your own weakness, and not diminish the dignity of the powerful, but understand the nature that is appropriate and fitting to God, and accept the words suitable to the humble. If we wished to deal with this subject accurately and in detail we would need an infinite number of words.

(2)

The Spirit transforms us

But let us return to the main subject. Once the mind has been purified of all desire for this world and has left behind every form of sentient life, rising up like a fish from the depths to the surface, it will now in the purity of its creation be able to see the Holy Spirit, the Father and the Son, who in the same nature and essence possess the same goodness, righteousness, holiness and life.

For scripture says: 'Your spirit is good', and 'Your spirit is virtuous'. And the apostle says: 'The life-giving law of the Spirit'. None of these is acquired or can come into existence at a later stage. For just as warmth cannot be separated from fire, nor brilliance from light, so the power to sanctify and to give life, together with the qualities of goodness and righteousness, cannot be separated from the Spirit. For it is here that the Spirit resides in its blessed being, where it cannot be numbered in the plural but appears only in the singularity of the Trinity, and is indivisible. For just as the Father is one and the Son is one, so too the Holy Spirit is one.

The ministers of the Spirit, however, seem to us to be beyond number in their particulars. Yet we should not look to creation for that which exists outside it, or judge the sanctity of that which sanctifies. For the Spirit fills the angels and archangels; he sanctifies their powers and gives all things life. The Spirit is spread throughout all creation and yet gives of his essence without ever being diminished in the process. He distributes his grace to everything, and yet is never dispersed in those particulars, but is constantly replenishing those he has visited without losing anything himself. For just as the sun shines on various things, giving of itself but never being diminished in the process, so the Spirit lavishes his gifts, while remaining complete and undivided. He lightens the path to God for all who seek it, inspiring the prophets, giving wisdom to the legislators and spiritual guidance to the priests. He gives strength to kings and confidence to the honest and just. He heals the sick and revives the dead, releasing those in chains and adopting those without a family. If he finds a tax-collector he makes a disciple; if he meets a fisherman he produces a theologian; if he finds a persecutor he makes an apostle who can spread the faith and be his chosen instrument. Through the working of the Spirit, the weak can escape the strong, the poor become rich and the ignorant surpass the wise.

Although Paul was weak, through the presence of the Spirit he was given the power to heal those who received items of his clothing. When Peter was surrounded by the sick, through the intervention of the Spirit, those his shadow fell upon were immediately cured of their illness. Peter and John were both poor men possessing neither gold nor silver and yet they were given the gift to heal, which is far more valuable than a heap of gold coins; for there was a lame man who had been given money by many but had remained a beggar, but once he had received Peter's gift he leaped up like a deer praising God and no longer had to beg. John who was ignorant of the wisdom of this world was able, thanks to the power of the Spirit, to express wisdom which surpassed that of the wisest.

The Spirit is in heaven, but he fills the world with his ubiquitous presence which cannot be constrained. He is wholly present in each, and yet wholly with God. He distributes gifts but not like any ordinary giver, for he does so under his own authority. As scripture says: 'He gives to each as he sees fit', making his dispensation with discretion and of his own free will. Let us pray that he is always at our side and that he never abandons us, by the grace of our Lord, Jesus Christ, whose power and glory is eternal. Amen.

(3)

an ascetic discourse

Freedom from passions

H uman beings were made in the image of God, but because of their sin the beauty of the image was destroyed and the soul dragged down by passionate desires. But God who made humanity is the true life. And so, as a consequence of humanity losing its likeness to God, it lost its harmony with life, since we cannot be outside God and still live a contented life.

Let us return to the original state of grace from which we were exiled by sin, making ourselves in the image of God once more, so that we may be like the Creator in our freedom from desire. For if you can make your life as close to the passionless calm of the divine nature as possible, then your soul will be restored to the image of God. And if you can achieve this similarity to God, you will also have attained the image of the divine life which lasts for ever in its eternal happiness.

If by our freedom from passions we can regain the image of God which will offer us eternal life, then let us ignore everything else while we concentrate on this object, so that our soul may never again be dominated by passion, and our mind may remain firm and unconquerable in the face of temptations, and thus we may share in God's blessedness.

Virginity, if it is understood in its spiritual sense, can be helpful in achieving this aim. For merely refusing to produce children is not true virginity, since you must be a virgin in the whole of your life and character, displaying the purity of the virgin in everything you do. For it is possible to commit fornication by speaking and adultery by looking, just as we can become polluted by what we hear and be defiled in our heart, or pass the limits of moderation by excessive eating or drinking. If you can show self-control within the rule of virginity, then you will find the grace of virginity in all its forms perfected within you.

(1)

Purity regards more than just the body

Therefore if we really want our soul to be like God, free from passion so that we may gain eternal life, let us look at our own life so that we do not break our promise and be condemned like Ananias. For Ananias would have been justified to begin with in not promising his property to God. He sought public praise, however, by promising to pledge it to God, hoping that he would be admired by everyone for his generosity. But, by withholding part of the price, he only succeeded in rousing the anger of God against him, through his apostle Peter, so that he could find no room to repent.

For this reason you are allowed, if you so wish, to follow the normal course of marriage, in accordance with what is legitimate, before taking up the religious life. Once you have made your decision, however, you must keep yourself for God like a holy votive-offering, so that you do not commit sacrilege by defiling the body which has been consecrated to God by a solemn promise in the ordinary actions of life. In saying this I am not thinking of just one form of vice, as some do, who consider that they can possess the virtue of virginity merely by tending to the body. Rather, I believe that we must consider every form of undesirable attitude since, if you want to stay close to God, you must not be sullied by any of the vices of this world. Anger, jealousy, revengefulness, deception, arrogance, loose thoughts, foolish talk, sloppiness in prayer, desire for things of no substance, neglect of the commandments, lavish dressing, cosmetics, irrelevant and unnecessary meeting and conversations: all these require just the same degree of vigilance on the part of those who have dedicated themselves to God in virginity, since the danger of falling into one of these is just as great as that of committing the forbidden sin.

For every time we fall victim to one of these undesirable attitudes, the purity of our soul is damaged and we depart from the divine life. Those who have renounced the world must be on their guard against these sorts of actions so that they do not pollute themselves, that is, God's vessels. For if you have chosen the life of angels, you have passed the confines of human nature and crossed over to the bodiless state. For the angelic nature is one free from the bonds of marriage, which thinks of no beauty except a continual gazing on the face of God. If you have raised yourself to the order of angels and then cover yourself with ordinary vices, you are like a leopard's skin, whose hair is neither pure white nor pure black, but is spotted with a mixture of both colours, and can be described neither as white nor black. This then is a general statement to those who have chosen the continent and holy life.

(2)

The good conduct of communal life

On particular points, however, we must add a few brief notes. Those who have chosen to remove themselves from the common life and are training for the divine life must not do so by themselves or without guidance. For such a life must have witnesses so that it will not attract unwelcome suspicions. For just as the spiritual law requires that those who eat the sacred passover should not be less than twelve, so the ten who practise the spiritual life together should be increased rather than diminished.

There should be one person to direct the community, chosen to lead by the example he has set in his life and character and his considered speech. The question of age should be borne in mind when selecting such a leader since it is natural for people to give greater respect to their seniors in age. He should have great authority and command the immediate obedience of all those under him, for nobody in the community should resist his will if it is conducive to a well-ordered and disciplined life. Just as the apostle says that we must not resist the powers ordained by God, since those who do will be punished, so here too the rest of the community should be reminded that the power given to the ruler is not arbitrary but is given by God to ensure that progress to him may be unhindered, provided that he gives them useful and beneficial advice and they accept this advice with immediate obedience.

And since it is of the utmost importance for the whole community to be receptive and obedient towards the leader, it is vital that the leader of this life should possess a character which may serve as an example of every virtue for those that look upon it, being, in the words of the apostle, 'temperate, fair-minded, disciplined, and able to teach'.

Thus I think that it is necessary to investigate his whole life and not just ensure that he is of the right age, for it is possible to find an immature character in someone with grey hair and wrinkles. In particular, you should see that his character and manners have matured in an agreeable fashion, so that everything he says and does may have the force of law and precedent for the community.

On the subject of food it is right that those who practise this life should follow the guidance of the apostle and work with their hands to eat their daily bread. This work should be undertaken under the supervision of an older person of serious and unimpeachable character who will arrange their manual work as required, observing the rule that bids us earn our food with sweat and toil, so that our behaviour may remain irreproachable, and we should never need to go outside the community to satisfy our daily needs.

We should endeavour to follow the rule of moderation, avoiding the excesses both of luxury and physical abuse, so our bodies are not ruined either by obesity or starvation in following the commandments. For both extremes can do equal harm, and so we must avoid letting our body get out of control by a life of ease, and abusing it so that it is made weak and unresponsive. For in both these states the soul is deprived of the time to look with freedom upon higher things, since it is distracted and obsessed by the sensation of pain, being dragged down to the level of the ill-used body.

(3)

Balance in monastic life

We should make use of things as we need them, never rejecting wine if it can be used for beneficial purposes, but avoiding unnecessary use of it. And similarly we should use other things to serve the needs rather than the desires of the community.

The whole of our life should be a season of prayer. Since, however, we must not break up the constant cycle of prayer, we must follow the hours of prayer prescribed by the saints. David says: 'At midnight I got up to give thanks to you for your righteous judgments'. And we find that both Paul and Silas follow this rule when they praised God in prison at midnight. The same prophet says: 'In the evening and in the morning and at midday'. Moreover, the coming of the Holy Spirit took place at the third hour, as we have learned from Acts; and when the Pharisees laughed at the disciples because the Spirit had spoken in many different tongues, Peter said that those who spoke in that way were not drunk because it was only nine in the morning. The ninth hour recalls the Lord's passion, which took place so that we might have life. But as David says: 'I praised you seven times a day because of your righteous judgments', and the times of prayer mentioned do not complete the seven hours for prayer, for we must divide the midday prayer and say part before and part after eating: so that in the whole course of the day we may fulfil the seven acts of daily worship in praise of God.

The gates of the monasteries must be closed to women, and only those men whom the Superior permits to enter may do so. For frequent visits give rise to inappropriate and foolish talk which then leads on to foolish and useless thoughts. And so it should be the general rule that when conversation is necessary, the Superior alone should be asked things and give the replies, and that the others should not answer any frivolous questions put to them by visitors lest they be distracted by idle talk.

There should be a common store-cupboard, and nobody should call anything their own, neither their coat, shoes, or anything else that the body requires. The Superior's authority should decide what use should be made of these things, dispensing to each according to his needs from the common store.

The law about love does not allow personal friendships within the community, since it is inevitable that personal affections will seriously disrupt the harmony of the whole. It is right that everyone should regard each other with an equal amount of affection, maintaining a single standard of love for the whole community. If anyone is found to have greater feelings of affection towards a fellow monk who is a brother, a kinsman, or no relation, then any excuse should be disregarded and he should be punished since he is damaging the whole community. For you cannot love a particular person without incurring a deficiency in your love for the rest.

The punishments of anyone who is condemned for any fault should be suited to the gravity of his sin: he may be excluded from singing, or from the communal prayers or from participation in meals. The monk who is assigned the keeping of discipline will decide on the punishment to suit the gravity of the offence.

The service of the whole community should be taken in rotation, two monks in succession for a week at a time performing all the necessary work, so that all may share in the rewards of humility, with no one being allowed to surpass the others in the performing of good work, and with everyone being allowed a rest. For if work and rest are taken in turn, the weary no longer feel tired.

The Superior of the community should have the power to send those he regards as suitable on journeys if they are necessary and make those for whom it is best to remain within the house stay there. For it must be remembered that when men are young, even if they take every possible care to ensure self-control, that the beauty inseparable from that age blossoms forth and offers temptation to those who encounter it. So if there are any men at the height of their physical beauty, they must be kept out of sight until their body assumes a more fitting appearance.

There must be no sign of anger or jealousy, or absence of forgiveness among the monks; nor any gesture, movement, word, look, expression or anything of that kind, calculated to annoy a companion. And if any should be found guilty of one of these, he shall not be allowed to plead provocation to excuse his sin. For wrong is wrong regardless of the circumstances under which it is done.

Every form of oath must be excluded from the ranks of the ascetics. A nod of the head or verbal assent may be counted as an oath, both by the speaker and the listener. If anyone thinks that this is not a sufficient guarantee, then he is condemning his own conscience by revealing his lack of truthfulness in conversation, and must be regarded as committing wrong by the Superior and therefore punished.

When the day is over and all work, both physical and spiritual, has come to an end, each man should examine his own conscience before he goes to sleep. And if he has done anything wrong, thinking forbidden thoughts, talking too much, being negligent in prayer, or inattentive in singing, or feeling a yearning for the outside world, then let him confess this sin to the whole community, so that his fault may be healed by the prayers of all.

(4–5)

from the longer rules

Obey Christ now

S ince, by the grace of God, we who have set as our common aim a life of piety are assembled in one place in the name of our Lord Jesus Christ, and since you so clearly want to learn about salvation, I feel I must speak about the righteous acts of God, remembering at all times the Apostle who said: 'For three years I never ceased night or day from warning each one of them with my tears'. The present is just the right time to begin this, especially as this place offers us peace and complete freedom from the disturbances of the outside world. And so let us pray together that all of us be given our daily bread, and that having received our advice you may be like fertile ground and bring forth the perfect fruit of justice in abundance, as it is written.

I ask you, therefore, by the grace of our Lord Jesus Christ who died for our sins, to show every concern for your soul. For we must repent for the vanity of our former life and strive for those things that will add to the glory of God, Christ, and the Holy Spirit. Let us abandon a dissolute life of ease and that slowness which ensures that we always miss the opportunity when it arises or put it off until tomorrow or the distant future: for otherwise we may be found wanting in just deeds by the one who demands our souls, and be thrown out of the bride-chamber, shedding vain and useless tears, and lamenting our ill-spent life, at a time when it is too late to repent.

The Apostle says: 'Now is the right time, now is the day of salvation'. Now is the time for us to repent, work, and show patience; in the future we shall find our reward, recompense, and comfort. It is in the present that God gives us help to avoid the path of evil, but in the future he will be a stern and inexorable examiner of all actions, words and thoughts. Now we may enjoy his gentle patience, but then we shall discover his justice when we shall rise again, some to eternal punishment, others to eternal life, and each shall receive according to their works.

How long should we put off our obedience to Christ, who has called us to his heavenly kingdom? Should we not try to receive the good fruit offered to us, changing our old habits so that we can live a life of integrity such as is shown to us by the gospels? Should we not always keep before our eyes that terrible appointed day of the Lord, when those who have lived a life full of just actions will come to the Lord's right hand and be received into the kingdom of heaven, while those who have not will be enveloped in the fire of hell and everlasting darkness? 'There', it says, 'will be the weeping and gnashing of teeth'.

(1)

Paradise gained by the virtuous

We claim that we desire the kingdom of heaven, and yet we neglect those things that ensure we could gain entry there. And although we make no efforts to fulfil the Lord's commands, we still imagine in our foolishness that we will receive the same honours as those who have fought against sin right up to their death. Who has ever stayed at home doing nothing at harvest-time and managed to fill his arms with bundles of corn? Who has ever gathered grapes from the vine he has not planted and worked hard for? Those who have worked receive the fruits, those who are victorious are crowned.

And who would begin to consider crowning anyone who had not even got ready to face his opponent? Yet it is not enough to be victorious since we must also make sure that we compete according to the rules, as the Apostle says; for we must not neglect even the smallest details of our instructions, but carry out our orders to the letter. For it is said: 'Blessed is that servant whom the Lord finds', not doing anything but, 'so doing'. And, 'If you have acted in the right way but have not shared out correctly, you have sinned'.

(2)

79

The imperative of living the Lord's Word

If any of you think that you are lacking in anything, you should bring it out in the open so that all of us may examine the case together. For it is easier for a group of people to find out what is hidden by careful scrutiny, since God ensures that we may find what we seek through the guidance and teaching of the Holy Spirit. And just as: 'Necessity forces me to preach the gospel, or suffer the consequences', so you too are in equal danger if you are backward in your search, or if you are careless and negligent in obeying your instructions, or in carrying them out by good works. For the Lord says: 'The word I have spoken will be the same one, that will judge you on the last day'. And, 'The servant who was ignorant of the Lord's will and did things that deserved punishment will receive only a light beating; but the one who knew and yet still disobeyed his Lord will receive a sound thrashing'.

Therefore let us pray that I may teach you the word without blame, and that it will bear fruit in you. And since we know that the words of the divine scriptures will rise up before us at the judgement seat of Christ, 'For I will reprove you', he says, 'and set your sins before you', let us take careful heed of that which is spoken, and seek to carry out God's orders. For we do not know on what day or at what hour the Lord will come.

(3)

The beauty of God

Now what is more marvellous than divine beauty? What thought could be more delightful than the magnificence of God? And what desire of the soul is as strong and overbearing as that which comes from God upon the soul that has been purified of all evil and cries with real affection, 'I am wounded by love'?

The flashes of divine beauty transcend all speech and description; words cannot express them nor hearing receive them. Although you can compare them to the beams of the morning star, or the brightness of the moon or the light of the midday sun, all such comparisons utterly fail to express the true nature of its light, for it is like comparing the profound darkness of a moonless night with the penetrating glare of the sun at noon.

True beauty is unseen by human eyes, and grasped only by the soul and the mind when it has happened to illuminate one of the saints, and left behind a wound of unbearable yearning. Saints who, weary of the present life, cried, 'Alas, that my stay here is prolonged'. And, 'When shall I come and appear before the presence of God?' And again, 'To depart and be with Christ, that would be the best'. And again, 'My soul thirsts for God, the strong, the living one'. And, 'Lord now let your servant depart'. For this life seemed like a prison to those souls who had been touched by a yearning for the divine so they were scarcely able to control their impulses. For they had an insatiable desire to see the beauty of the divine and prayed that their contemplation of God's love might continue in the eternal life.

So then by our human nature we desire beauty. But the good is properly fair and worthy of love. Now God is good and all things desire good. Therefore all things desire God.

(3)

Detached from all and mindful of God

Anyone who truly wants to follow God must be free from the bonds of attachment to this life. To do this we must make a complete break with our old way of life. Indeed, unless we avoid all obsession with the body and with the concerns of this world, we shall never succeed in pleasing God. We must depart as it were to another world in our way of thinking, as the Apostle said: 'Our citizenship is in heaven'. For the Lord said quite clearly: 'Any of you who does not renounce everything he has cannot be my disciple'.

Once we have managed to achieve this, we must remain ever on our guard to ensure that we never lose the thought of God, or destroy the memory of his wonders with our wandering minds. For we must keep the pure thought of God continually imprinted in our souls, as if it were an indelible seal.

For in this way we may gain the love of God, which both stirs us to carry out the Lord's commandments and is preserved by them in security for ever. The Lord said: 'If you love me, keep my commandments', and in another place: 'If you keep my commandments, you shall remain loved by me', adding with still more insistence: 'Even as I have kept my father's commandments and abide in his love'.

(5)

Doing God's will is recollection of him

And so he teaches us to work according to the will of him who gave the commandments, and to direct all our efforts towards him, as he says elsewhere: 'I have come down from heaven not to do my own will, but the will of my Father who sent me'. For just as the various activities required in our daily life have their own objects and their respective ways of being done, so also there is one rule and canon prescribed for all our works, which is to fulfil God's commandments according to his will. Hence it is impossible for our work to be done properly unless it is carried out in obedience to the will of him who has prescribed it.

By taking care to do our work as God wills, we shall be linked to God in memory. The smith in making an axe considers the person who set this task, having them in his thoughts at all times, so he can plan the right shape and size by directing his work according to the wishes of the one who commissioned it. For if he does not keep his patron in mind, he will produce something other than or different from what he set out to make.

In the same way, Christians, directing all their energies small and great to the fulfilling of God's will, at one and the same time accomplish the work carefully and preserve the intention of him who gave the order and fulfil what was said: 'I have seen the Lord before me at all times, for he is on my right hand, lest I be shaken'. And they do what they have been commanded: 'Whether you eat or drink or whatever you do, do all to the glory of God.'

(6)

a discourse on ascetic discipline

How the monk must be equipped

The first requirement for those who wish to follow the monastic life is that they must possess nothing. Next they must ensure that they find solitude, dress simply and keep their speech and tone of voice within the bounds of moderation. Their tranquillity must not be disturbed by eating or drinking, which must be done in silence. They must maintain silence in the presence of their elders, listening to those who are wiser than they are, showing love to their equals, and giving advice to those below them in a spirit of charity. They must avoid contact with the sort of people who like causing trouble, and instead think deeply and say little. In their speech they must avoid both arrogance and idle chatter, avoiding easy laughter and maintaining a sense of shame. They must keep their eyes fixed on the ground and their soul directed above, refusing to argue with those who have contradicted them. They must show obedience, do manual work, and never forget the true purpose of their life, but rejoice in hope, showing patience in difficult times. They must pray constantly, giving thanks for everything, being humble towards all and avoiding arrogance. They must remain sober and keep their heart free from evil things, laying up treasure in heaven by keeping the commandments, and constantly scrutinizing their daily thoughts and actions. They must keep themselves away from the world of business and other useless engagements with this world, avoiding a life of ease, and seek to imitate the life of the holy fathers. They must feel joy for those who manage to live the life of virtue and not be envious of them, showing compassion for those who are suffering by sharing their tears and grief, and never seeking to blame them. They should not reproach anyone who has turned away from a life of sin, or seek self-justification but rather confess before God and other people that they themselves are the greater sinners. They must reproach the slovenly, giving encouragement to the faint-hearted and support to the weak. They must wash the feet of the saints, show hospitality and love, finding peace in the company of those who share the faith, avoiding heretics, reading the canonical books and never even opening the apocryphal ones. They must not argue about the Father, Son, and Holy Spirit, but speak and think confidently about the Trinity, uncreated and of a single substance. If they are questioned on this matter they must reply that it is necessary to be baptized according to the tradition, to believe as we have been baptized, and to worship as we believe. They must occupy their time with good works and speech, never swearing, or lending money at interest, or trying to make a profit from their corn, wine and oil. They should avoid any excess in eating or drinking, keep out of business, and never lie or slander anyone. They must never seek to diminish anyone, or take pleasure from listening to anyone doing it, nor be ready to believe rumour. They should not be overcome by anger or despondency, nor should they be quick to get angry or be slow to be appeased, nor return evil with evil. Instead they must be prepared to be slandered rather than commit slander, to be struck rather than strike, and be cheated rather than cheat.

Above all, a monk must avoid all contact with women and wine, since they can lead even the wise astray. And in keeping the commandments to the best of their ability, they must not give in to listlessness, but await their reward and praise from God and long for the enjoyment of eternal life, never forgetting the words of David who said: 'I have seen the Lord before me at all times, for he is on my right hand, lest I be shaken'. They must love God with all their heart and strength, and mind and power, like a child. And like a slave, they must respect and fear him and obey him, working for their salvation with fear and trembling. They must show spiritual strength, be clothed in the Holy Spirit, advancing with confidence, and fighting with purpose and effect, so that they may defeat their enemy in the weakness of their flesh and the poverty of their soul, carrying out God's commandments while confessing that they themselves are useless. They should give thanks to the holy glory and terror of God, doing nothing to create strife or self-praise, and everything to win the pleasure of God. 'For God has scattered the bones of those who have sought only their own pleasure'. They should not boast, praising themselves or delighting when they hear their praises sung by others. They must do their work inconspicuously and without show, seeking only the praise that comes from God, and remembering his terrifying and glorious arrival, when they will leave this place and either enjoy the good things stored up for the just or suffer the fire prepared for the devil and his angels. And, in addition, they should remember the apostolic doctrine: 'The sufferings of the present are as nothing in comparison with the glory that will be revealed to us in the time to come'. They should look to the future and say with David: 'For those who keep his commandments there is a great reward'; a mighty reward, crowns of righteousness, eternal dwellings, endless life, inexpressible joy, and indestructible life with the Father and the Son and the Holy Spirit, the true God in heaven, revealed to you directly, choruses in company with the angels, fathers, patriarchs, prophets, apostles, martyrs, confessors, and those who have pleased God from the beginning.

Let us strive to be found in this company, by the grace of our Lord Jesus Christ, to whom is glory and dominion for ever. Amen.

(1–2)

on the holy spirit

The names of Christ

Through the Son comes every kind of help for the soul, and each manner of his care has been given its own proper name. So when he draws the unblemished soul to himself, which has neither spot nor stain, like a pure virgin, he is called the Bridegroom. But when he receives and cures the soul who is afflicted with the evil strokes of the devil and weighed down by sin, then he is called Physician.

But shall his concern for us debase the way that we think of him? Or shall it have the opposite effect by inspiring amazement in us at the great power and love for humanity of our Saviour, who both allowed himself to suffer our infirmities with us and was able to come down to our condition of weakness. For neither heaven nor earth, nor the immensity of the oceans, nor the creatures that live in the water or on the dry land, neither plants, stars, air, nor the seasons, nor even the abundant variety of the cosmic order can show so well the supremacy of his might as the fact that the infinite God should have been able unsufferingly to face death through the flesh, so that by his own suffering we might be granted freedom from suffering. The Apostle says: 'In all these things we are more than conquerers through him who loved us'. But in this phrase there is no suggestion of any lowly and

95

subordinate ministry, but rather of the help rendered in the strength of his might.

And, insofar as all created things, both visible and of the mind, need the care of God to sustain them, the Creator Word, the only-begotten God, grants help according to the need of each, distributing his benefits which are as various and numerous as are those who receive them.

To those confined in the darkness of ignorance he brings light, for which reason he is the True Light. Measuring out just returns, he judges, and is therefore the Just Judge. 'For the Father judges no one, but has committed all judgement to the Son'. He raises up from their fallen state those who have slipped from the heights of life into sin, for which reason he is the Resurrection. He works all things by the touch of his power and the will of his goodness. He shepherds, he enlightens, he nourishes, he guides, he heals, he raises up. He calls into being those things which were not and he sustains in being those things which are.

Thus the good things of God come to us through the Son who works in each case with greater speed than tongue can tell. For neither lightning, nor the passage of light through the air, is so swift, and neither is the glance of the eye, nor the movement of our thought. But the divine energy surpasses each of these by as much as the most sluggish of creatures is surpassed in speed by the birds, or the winds, or the forward movement of the planets or, indeed, by thought itself.

The Spirit of God

First of all, who is not uplifted in their soul when they hear the titles of the Spirit, and who does not raise their minds to the Supreme Being? For he is called the 'Spirit of God', and the 'Spirit of Truth who proceeds from the Father', the 'right Spirit' and the 'guiding Spirit', though his proper and legitimate name is 'Holy Spirit', which is most particularly the name of all that is incorporeal, wholly immaterial and indivisible. Thus our Lord, when he taught the woman who believed that we should worship God in one place that the incorporeal is incomprehensible, said: 'God is Spirit'.

When we hear of a spirit, then it is impossible to conceive of a circumscribed nature, subject to change and variation, just like a creature. But we approach the all-highest with our minds and are compelled to conceive of an intelligent essence of unlimited power and infinite magnitude, unmeasured by times or epochs, generous in the bestowing of good things, one turned to by all things needing sanctification, desired by all things living in virtue, and they are watered by his inspiration and helped on towards their natural and proper end.

He perfects all other things but himself lacks nothing; not needing restoration of life, he bestows life; not gradually growing, but complete, established in himself, and everywhere present. He is the origin of sanctification, the light of intelligence, supplying illumination through himself to every mind enquiring after truth. He is inaccessible to nature, comprehended by its goodness, filling all things with his power, communicated only to those who are worthy, not shared out in a single measure but distributed in his energy according to the extent of a person's faith.

He is simple in his essence and various in his powers, wholly present in each individual and wholly present everywhere; he is divided without feeling pain and is shared out without ceasing to be whole, like the rays of the sun whose goodness falls on the person who enjoys it as if it existed for them alone, and yet it illumines the earth and the seas and penetrates the air. This too is how the Holy Spirit is for whoever receives him, as though given to them alone, and yet he pours forth sufficient and undiminished grace on all and is enjoyed by all who share in him, according to the capacity not of his power but of their nature.

The Paraclete

The Spirit is not united to the soul by spacial proximity (for how could that which has no body be approached by a body?), but rather by the departure of the passions which came upon the soul on account of its friendship with the body and which have alienated it from its fellowship with God.

Only when someone has been purified from the shame which they contracted through vice, and has returned to the original beauty of their own nature, purifying the Royal Image and returning it to its original form, is it possible for them to draw near to the Paraclete. And he, like the sun, will show to your purified eye the image in himself of the invisible God, and in the blessed sight of the image you will behold the unspeakable beauty of the archetype.

Through him hearts are raised up, the weak are led by the hand, and those who are making progress are perfected. He shines upon those who are cleansed of all stain and makes them spiritual by fellowship with himself. Just as brilliant and radiant objects, when touched by a sunbeam, become brighter still and themselves emit an even greater radiance, so too spirit-bearing souls are illumined by the Spirit and themselves become spiritual and send forth their grace for others.

From this there comes foreknowledge of what is to be, the understanding of mysteries, the perception of what is hidden, the distribution of charismatic gifts, the citizenship of heaven, a place with angel choirs, unending joy, abiding in God, being made like God and, highest of all, becoming God. These then are just a few of our ideas concerning the Holy Spirit, which we have been taught to hold regarding his greatness, his dignity and his operations by the utterances of that same Spirit.

The fullness of the Spirit

Through the Holy Spirit comes our return to paradise, our ascent to the kingdom of heaven, our adoption again as sons and daughters of God, our freedom to call God Father, our sharing in the grace of Christ, our being called children of light, our part in eternal glory; in a word, our coming into the fullness of the blessing, in this world and in the world to come, of those good things stored up for us in promises, which, beholding their grace as in a mirror, we anxiously await through faith as though they were already present. If this is the pledge, then how great is the final reward? If these are the first fruits, then how great is the fullness?

The power of the Spirit

But what are the functions of the Holy Spirit, which are ineffable on account of their magnitude and in-numerable on account of their multitude? How can we conceive of what extends beyond the ages? What were his functions before that creation of which we *can* conceive? How great were the benefits he bestowed upon the creation? What power did he have over the ages that were to come?

He existed, he pre-existed and co-existed with the Father and the Son before the ages. And so if you can conceive of what extends beyond the ages, then you will find the Spirit beyond even that. And if you think of the creation, then the powers of the heavens were established by the Spirit, their establishment residing in the fact that they were not able to depart from the good. For it is by the Spirit that the powers have their fellowship with God, their not being able to turn to evil and their remaining in permanent blessedness.

Then there is the incarnation of Christ, of which the Spirit was the forerunner. His coming was in the flesh, but the Spirit was inseparable. The working of miracles and gifts of healing are performed through the Holy Spirit. Demons are exorcised in the Spirit of God. The devil is brought low by the presence of the Spirit. Sins are forgiven by the grace of the Spirit, for 'You were washed, you were sanctified, you were justified in the name of the Lord Jesus Christ and in the Spirit of our God'.

The Spirit bestows fellowship with God, for 'God has sent the Spirit of his Son into our hearts, crying,

"Abba! Father!" ' The raising of the dead is an operation of the Spirit, for 'When you send forth your Spirit, they are created; and you renew the face of the earth'. If we understand creation here to mean the bringing to life of those who have died, then how great is the operation of the Spirit who dispenses life to us from resurrection and transforms the soul in harmony with that spiritual life to come! But our souls are raised to the most intense admiration, if creation means a change for the better in those who have fallen into sin here below (for this can be its meaning in scripture, as when Paul says: 'Therefore, if anyone is in Christ, he is a new creation'), a change that means renewal in this life and the transformation from our earthly existence of the passions to the heavenly way of being, which comes about through the Spirit.

In view of all these things, should we really fear that we might go beyond the proper limits in the honour we give the Spirit? Or should we fear rather that we may belittle him, about whom we seem to have the highest human thoughts and to give the greatest of names?

Selected letters

To his friend Gregory

S olitude offers us an excellent opportunity for calm-
ing our passions and giving our reason time to
remove them thoroughly from our soul. For just as
wild animals can be soothed by being stroked, so all
our anger, fear and stress, which poison and disrupt
our soul, can be soothed by an atmosphere of peace
where the freedom from constant disturbance ensures
that our soul can be brought more easily under the
power of reason. We should look for a place we can
make entirely our own, away from contact with other
people, so that our spiritual training may progress on
an uninterrupted path, feeding our soul with thoughts
of God. There is nothing better than to imitate here on
earth the choir of angels: beginning the day by offering
prayers and hymns in honour of the Creator, and then
when the rays of the sun shine forth, going about our
work to the accompaniment of prayers and hymns to
lighten our tasks. For the singing of hymns brings joy
and removes pain from our soul. Tranquillity is the
first step in the purification of our soul, when we
no longer speak of human matters, ceasing to look
around in search of finely proportioned bodies, or
dissipating the harmony of the soul by being drawn
to enticing sounds or being distracted by elegant and
witty words which cause the greatest disturbance to

the soul's energy. For the spirit which is not scattered on the outside and diffused by the senses into the world, returns to itself, and sets out from there to be one with God; and then, brilliant and resplendent with divine beauty, it begins to forget its own nature, giving no thought to food or clothing which distract the soul but, taking leave of all mundane, ordinary concerns, it concentrates its whole being on attaining eternal goods. There can surely be no better way than this to realize moderation and courage, justice and prudence, and all those other virtues in their various subdivisions which guide decent people in the proper conduct of their life.

II

The best guide you can find to the correct path is the serious study of the Bible. There we can find rules for the conduct of our life and, in the lives of great figures, living images of a life with God whose actions we are encouraged to copy. Each person can concentrate on the area where they feel themselves to be lacking and find, as in a hospital, a cure for their particular trouble. Thus someone who looks for self-control should read and re-read the story of Joseph, and so learn how to practise self-control and discover not only the strength Joseph showed in the face of desire, but also how firmly he was disposed to virtue. Courage can be learnt by following the example of Job. Here was a man who suffered a complete reversal of fate and, having once been rich and the father of numerous children, was reduced in a single moment to poverty and childlessness. And yet he managed to remain completely unchanged, never ceasing to attend to the well-being of his soul and even showing anger towards those friends of his who had come to console him but who ended up by insulting him and merely increasing his afflictions. If anyone is seeking to become kind yet firm so that they can be steadfast against sin while being gentle towards others, then they should look at the example set by David who managed to be strong in the midst of battle and yet kind and compassionate in his responses to his enemies. Moses too showed such qualities when he displayed great anger towards those who sinned against God, but was tolerant towards those who slandered himself. And just as painters produce an image by referring to another, constantly shifting their gaze from their model to their own work in an attempt to transfer its features into their own work of art, so those who seek to perfect themselves in every aspect of virtue should look to the lives of the saints, which are like living and breathing works of art, and thus by imitation try to reproduce their virtues in their own life.

III

When we return to prayer after a period of reading
we find a rejuvenated and envigorated soul, stirred
by the desire for God. The best form of prayer is
one that implants the clearest idea of God in the
soul and thus makes space for the presence of God
within us. We become a temple of God when our
continuous meditation on him is not constantly in-
terrupted by ordinary worries, and the spirit is not
disturbed by unexpected emotions. Thus, in flight
from all things, the spirit who loves God can approach
God who drives out everything that leads us to evil, and
holds steadfastly to everything that leads to virtue.

IV

Above all we should strive not to be ignorant of the way that we use language. We should make sure that we are not aggressive in how we ask questions and give our replies without seeking to show off. We should not interrupt when someone has something useful to say, nor be eager to make an ostentatious contribution, but rather try to observe a due measure both in listening and in speaking. We should not be too proud to learn nor too grudging to share the knowledge we possess. And if we have learnt something from someone else, then we should not try to conceal its true origin and act like those bad women who falsely try to pass off their children as legitimate, but rather we should declare the true author of the idea without favour. A moderate tone of voice ought to be adopted: neither so faint that it cannot be heard nor too strong so that it exhausts our listeners. Anyone who is going to speak in public should do so only after they have given careful consideration to what they are going to say. We must strive to be easy-going in conversation and agreeable in company, not seeking to enjoy ourselves by being witty but rather to produce sympathy by our good-natured encouragement. And in no circumstances should we show harshness, even when we have occasion to criticize someone.

To a widow on the baptism of her son

There is a technique for catching doves which is as follows: when one of the followers of this sport has managed to lay hold of a dove, they tame it and get it used to eating in their company. And then when they have poured perfume onto its wings, they set it free so it can rejoin the rest of its flock. The fragrance of the perfume ensures that the wild doves become the possession of the owner of the tame dove, because the sweet-smelling bird attracts the others which then follow it.

You may, perhaps, be wondering why I have begun my letter in this way? The point is that having taken your son, Dionysius, once called Diomedes, I have annointed the wings of his soul with divine perfume, and have sent him ahead in your honour, so that you too may be able to fly with him and come to the resting place set aside for us, of which I spoke to you before. If I live to see you too baptized, then your son will really have merited great reward.

Advice to the young

Since you have a life of solitude, full of faith and piety, you must learn how to live in accordance with the gospels, exercising control over your body, maintaining the humility of your spirit, the purity of your thought and keeping your anger in check. If you are conscripted, then use this to the service of God. If you are robbed, do not go to law. Show love towards hatred and tolerance towards persecution. And if you are slandered then respond with gentleness. Be as death to sin and crucify yourself for God. Concentrate all your concerns on the Lord so that you may find a place among the countless numbers of angels, the gatherings of the first born, the thrones of the apostles, the seats of the prophets, the sceptres of the patriarchs, the garlands of the martyrs and the praises of the just. You too should show every desire to ensure that you can be numbered among the just, in Christ Jesus, our Lord. Glory to him everlasting. Amen.

To a lapsed monk

If you still have any hope for your salvation remaining, if you have retained even the slightest thought of God, if you have any desire for the joys of the future or any terror of the tortures reserved for the impenitent, then come to your senses at once and lift up your eyes to heaven. Abandon this perversity, shake off this madness which has enveloped you and show some resistance to this force which is casting you down. Pick yourself up from the ground and remember the good shepherd who will come looking for you and restore you. If you still have two legs and the means to hear, then abandon this source of pain. Remember the compassion of the Lord when he tends us with oil and wine. Do not give up all hope for your salvation. Remember what is written: those who fall shall rise again, those who turn away shall be restored, those who have been beaten shall be looked after, those who are trapped by wild beasts shall survive, those who confess shall not be forsaken.

The Lord does not want the sinner to die but wishes him to repent and find life. Do not feel contempt because you have fallen into the depths of disaster. For this is the time of opportunity when you must think deeply and begin your recovery and return to health. If you have fallen then pick yourself up, if you have sinned then you must repent. Do not remain on the path of sin but get off it. Once you have been corrected and have groaned in pain, then you will be saved, for it is only after sweat and toil that you can

115

be restored to health and find salvation. Make sure that in your zeal to respect certain contracts you have made with others you do not neglect to honour those contracts you made to God in the presence of many witnesses. Do not hesitate for any human reasons to approach me. . . .

Do not let yourself be beaten. Remember the old days. Salvation and restitution are still open to you. Have courage, do not despair. There is no law to consign you to a pitiless death, but there is grace to save you from punishment and offer you the chance to be restored. The doors are not yet closed to you, the virgin is still listening, the sin is not yet in control. Take up the fight once more and feel pity for yourself and for all of us in Jesus Christ our Lord in whom is power now and forever. Amen.

To Urbicius, a monk

Y ou were intending to pay us a visit (and you were about to arrive) to offer us a little relief in all our troubles. And do you remember what happened? Our sins got in your way, preventing your landing so that we had to struggle on without your help.

Just as with waves, where no sooner has one broken than another is poised and threatens to swallow us in its dark mass, so with our troubles: the moment one is over, another is already looming over us. For most of the time there is only one answer, to yield to the moment and escape what immediately threatens.

But sometimes there seems to be virtually nothing that can offer us consolation and advice or can comfort us with mutual support. The most important thing is to pray continually so that we are not overcome by the great waves of trouble besetting us, but remember the grace of God. And if we do this we shall not be numbered among those fickle servants who believe when things are going well, but rebel when they are tested by adversity. And so let us use the present difficulties to our advantage, showing a greater faith in God since we have greater need of him.

To Evagrius, a priest

The great length of your letter did not bore me in the least, indeed I enjoyed it so much that it actually seemed quite short. For there is no news that could bring as much joy to a Christian as the news of peace, and there is nothing that would be more pleasing to God than this. May God reward you for the fine and strenuous efforts you are making in this splendid work of peacemaking. And remember, dear friend, that we are unceasing in our prayers to see the day on which we will all be able to be of one single and undivided mind in the same assembly, and in our desire to achieve this we will give way to nobody. We should indeed be the strangest of people if we were to find any pleasure in the schisms and divisions that beset the Church, and if we did not consider it as the greatest achievement to see the scattered limbs of Christ reassembled once more. Our desire to achieve this is as strong as the knowledge of our weakness to do so. Someone of your great wisdom will know only too well that difficulties having been aggravated by the passage of time will require time to correct them, and that it will take great perseverance and determination if we are to root out these evils entirely and so restore the sick to health. I am confident you will understand exactly what I mean even if I could have expressed myself with greater clarity.

To Eupaterius and his daughter

I was delighted to receive your fine letter not least because you manage to produce such a complete picture of yourself in what you wrote. For someone who wishes to mix with people who love God and benefit by this association, the arrival of such a letter conveying so much understanding of God can only be the greatest of pleasures. If Christ is our life then it follows that all our speech should be about him and that everything we do and think should be guided by his teaching, so that our soul should be formed in his image. I am delighted to be questioned on such subjects and pleased to be asked. In short, we place the profession of faith made by the Fathers at Nicaea over all those which came after, where it was agreed that the Son was consubstantial with the Father and of the same nature as he who had produced him. Light from Light, God from God, Good from Good, and all those attributes which the holy Fathers agreed upon and which have been attested by those of us who are following in their footsteps.

To the clergy at Samosata

The Lord dispenses everything for us in due measure and proportion, never burdening us with pain more than we can bear, but testing the strength of our faith by difficult circumstances that do not exceed our ability to endure. He adds a measure of tears in the water of those who must show that they can keep their faith in God in the midst of trouble. And he shows his love of us in not allowing our enemies to persecute us so much that the beatings we suffer would be able to shake us from our faith in Christ. It is by confronting you with enemies who can be easily conquered that he is preparing you for the victory you will win and the prize of your endurance. But the common enemy of our life is one who uses his own methods against the goodness of God and who, when he sees that you have denied any assault on your fortifications from outside, sees a means of insinuating into your midst the seeds of division and meanness. These are both harmless and easily dealt with at the beginning, but with the passage of time they multiply themselves by causing dissension until they become an incurable affliction. This is the reason for my sending you this letter, although I would have preferred to have seen you in person if it had been possible. But since circumstances do not permit this, I am sending you a letter begging you to take my advice to heart so that, having sorted out your differences, you will be able to inform me of the good news that your quarrels have been settled once and for all.

You ought to realize that you would be of far higher

stature before God if you displayed some humility before him, and accepted without shame the accusations made against you, even if they are not true, for the sake of peace. This would be a great help and would please the Church of God. If afterwards there is still some rivalry among you, then you should turn it to good use and, by your efforts to establish peace, strive to be worthy of being called a child of God.

And so we call on you to put aside all your internal struggles, which are only serving to delight our enemies and damage the reputation of your Church by being made public. You must act as if you were a single soul and heart living within a single body. It is the whole people of God, all its ministers and clergy, whom we embrace through your piety, and whom we call upon to be one with each other. We are not asking for anything more from them because in the past they have always shown the highest degree of willingness by setting an example in their actions.

To the people of Beraea

We have already had news of you, my dear friends, because of your deep devotion and the prize you have won by your faith in Christ. Perhaps one of you is wondering whether news of this has travelled abroad? The Lord himself makes sure that those who show outstanding faith are put in a prominent place as if they were a beacon whose light must shine over the whole world. Indeed, is it not the prize of victory that marks out the winners in the contest, and the conception of the work that shows the workman's skills? Now if achievements of this kind are never forgotten, then surely the Lord who has said 'I glorify those who glorify me' shall celebrate the actions of those who have shown great faith in Christ and shall display their glory before all, like the bright rays of the sun? Our love for you has been strengthened by the letter you sent us which reveals not only the previous struggles you have had to retain your piety, but also your rich resources of inner strength and true faith. We rejoice and pray with you that the God of us all, for whom we work and who hands out the prizes in the arena of life, will send you courage and strengthen your soul and bring your work to his side where it can find perfect recognition.

To Eustathius of Sebasteia

I had wasted much of my time and devoted almost all of my youth in acquiring knowledge which now appears as just foolishness before God. Then one day I awoke suddenly, as if from some deep sleep, and saw the intense light of divine truth, and realized the absolute worthlessness of all the wisdom taught by the leaders in this world. I wept many tears for the wretchedness of my life and prayed for some guidance to lead me to the life of faith. The first thing I did to reform my previous way of life was to mix with the poor. Having read the Bible, I thought that the best way to begin my road to perfection would be to buy food and possessions and distribute them among those of our brothers and sisters who had nothing. And, putting the usual concerns and troubles of this world completely out of my mind, I looked for people who would be willing to join me on this path and with whom I could navigate the great ocean of life. I found many such people in Alexandria and Egypt, and others in Palestine, Syria, and Mesopotamia. I was struck by their moderation in eating, their capacity for hard work, and the way they could banish sleep by prayer. Indeed, they seemed able to resist any force of nature, always giving complete and undivided attention to their soul, even if they were suffering hunger or thirst, or were cold and naked. They never gave in to their body or wasted the slightest attention on it, but seemed to be living in some other sphere and showed by their actions what it meant to be a stranger here on earth and a citizen in the heavenly state. The life of these people filled me with joy and amazement since they revealed that they were carrying within themselves the body of Christ. And so I decided that, as far as I was able, I too would try and follow their example.

To Eusebius, Bishop of Samosata

I t is not with the intention of increasing your troubles that we often include the description of our own grievances in letters to your honour, but rather that by airing them we may find some consolation. For once our deepest grief has been expressed it tends to be made more bearable. It is also to encourage you in your magnanimity to pray even harder for the Church. Moses had to pray for his people without ceasing, indeed in the battle against Amalek the saint kept his hands raised in prayer from dawn to dusk until the battle was finally won.

To the people of Evaesae

My dear friends, even though we are small and insignificant we are nevertheless all equal before the grace of God, which can never be altered by events. For there is not one faith at Seleucia, another at Constantinople, one at Zela, one at Lampsacus, and one at Rome; and those in the surrounding area are not different from these but are one and the same. We have all been baptized as we were taught by God, we have faith as we are baptized, and we worship God as we have faith. We do not separate the Holy Spirit from the Father or the Son nor claim that he is more important than the Father or older than the Son as certain heretics try to claim. Who would dare to reject the laws of God and think up their own order of priority for his names? We are not claiming the Holy Spirit was created after the Father and the Son nor that his role as our guide should be somehow subordinated. Indeed, we remind you of those words which the Lord spoke when he said: 'Every sin and blasphemy you commit will be forgiven except that against the Holy Spirit which will not be forgiven either now or in the time to come'.

Be on your guard against blasphemy towards the Holy Spirit. Remain steadfast in your faith and, as you look around the whole Church, remember that only a fraction of it is sick. All the rest of it, even to its furthest extent, has received the good news, and accepts this good and correct doctrine which we teach. And so we pray that we are not thrown out from their communion and that we will be together on the day of judgement when our Lord Jesus Christ dispenses our fate in accordance with our works.

To Palladius on his baptism

The good Lord has fulfilled exactly half my wish by ensuring that I should happen to meet your dear wife. He would fulfil the rest if I were able to see your own good self, which really would put me seriously in debt to the grace of God. I am especially eager to see you because I have heard how you have received the highest honour, that immortal covering which in enveloping our person completely destroys our mortal body since the mortal is absorbed within the immortal part. And so since, by the grace of God, you have been made one of his intimates, whom he has freed from sin, opening the gates of the heavenly palace for you and showing you the paths that lead to that blessed place, we call on you, who exceed all in your wisdom, to accept this grace and trust with due thought and see to it that you guard this royal treasure entrusted to you with the care it deserves. And then afterwards, if you have kept the seal undamaged, you will be able to stand beside the Lord gleaming in the light of the saints, without a mark or blemish on the robe of your immortality, retaining in each of your limbs that sanctity as one who is dressed in Christ. As it says in the Bible: 'All those who are baptized are clothed in Christ'. May all our limbs be sacred, so that they may be worthy of being covered in this holy robe of light.

To some monks

I am sure, by the grace of God, that I do not need to add anything further after what we have said to you in calling you all to embrace the communal life such as the apostles lived. You have received such advice as a form of wholesome instruction for which you ought to give thanks to God. The advice we have given you is a practical programme intended not just for your use but for our peace and to glorify and praise Christ in whose name we are called.

It is for this purpose that I have sent our dearest brother who will recognize those who are enthusiastic and rouse those who are lagging behind, informing us of any of you who are opposing our wishes. For we have, in short, a great desire to see you united, and to hear of your wish to live the life of a true witness, ensuring you remain vigilant in the pursuit of a life which bears witness to virtue. And so each of you will receive one reward for himself and another for the progress of his brother, for it is right that we should work for our mutual benefit in what we do and say according to our instructions.

But above all we must remind you of the faith of the Fathers so that dissension does not arise during a period of calm. However, you must realize that to follow your instructions to the letter is not in itself of benefit unless it is accompanied by faith in God. And similarly a correct confession without any good deeds will not be able to put you in God's presence. Both must be united for the human and the Divine to be as one and our life not to be crippled by deficiency. Faith will save us provided, as the Apostle says: 'It is revealed in our acts of charity'.

To Urbicius, a monk, on continence

You are right to think that we must define our subject to include not only continence but also its fruit. For the fruit is the participation in God. To ensure that it is preserved is to participate in God, just as to lose it is to participate in the life of the world. Continence means being repelled by the body and drawn to God. It distances itself from everything mortal as if its body were the Spirit of God, bringing us close to God by removing our envy and jealousy. Anyone who loves their body desires something that is not theirs, and if they can remove the disease of corruption from their heart they will find themselves fortified against every form of suffering because the body is death while life is immortal. If I understand the matter correctly, God can be said to be continence because he desires nothing and is completely self-sufficient. He does not desire what he sees or hears, yet lacks nothing and is filled with everything. Desire means that the soul is sick, while continence means the soul is healthy.

However, we should not deal with continence in just one of its spheres, in sexual desire for example, but examine all the ways in which desire damages the soul by thrusting it beyond necessity. There is desire for money and countless other unwelcome urges arising from other causes. There is the continence of not getting drunk or of not eating until we are about to burst, just as there is the continence of controlling our body and bad intentions. Often our soul is disturbed by a corrupt and false idea that divides our heart into many empty thoughts. Continence offers us true freedom in every way by looking after us and giving us power. It does not so much teach temperance as produce it. For the grace of God is temperance.

Consolation for the wife of Nectarius

I was not going to say anything to you out of respect for your dignity, knowing that for an inflamed eye even the gentlest of remedies will be painful, and similarly that for a soul burdened by a heavy grief even words of consolation can be unwelcome if they come at such a difficult time. But then I remembered that I was speaking to a Christian with a deep understanding of God and the world, for whom I should not fail in my duty.

I understand the pains that mothers have to experience and, knowing your own loving kindness, I realize how much you must be suffering in the present circumstances. For you have lost a son who, when he was alive was loved by every mother so much that they wished he was theirs, and now that he is dead they feel that they are burying one of their own. His death has affected two countries, ours and that of the Cilicians. With him the whole illustrious race collapsed as if, with his fall, it had suffered an earthquake. How terrible was the arrival of an evil spirit, what disastrous powers there are! Pity the earth which had to bear such a demon. The sun would shrink in terror before such a sight. How can we express the powerlessness of the soul?

We know that providence plays a part in our lives, for in the Bible it says that not even the fall of a single sparrow happens without our Father's wish. And so anything that takes place does so according to the will of our Creator. Who can oppose the will of God? And so let us accept what happens, for if we react with anger we will be unable to cope with whatever happens and will ourselves be destroyed. Let us not question the correctness of God's judgement, for we are powerless to understand his mysterious decisions. God is putting your love for him to the test. Now is the time for you to behave like the martyrs in showing patience. The mother of the Maccabees saw the death of seven sons and yet did not groan or give way to tears, but thanked God for delivering them from the fires, the steel and the torments of the flesh; for she felt honoured by God and other people. The trial is great but, I assure you, great are the rewards that God has reserved for those who suffer it with patience.

For when you became a mother and looked at your child praising God, you knew that you were mortal and you had given birth to a mortal. Why is it so strange that a mortal should die? Our grief is caused by its prematureness. We cannot say that it was premature, however, since we do not choose the right time for the soul, nor can we know what are the limits of human life.

Look around at the world in which you live and remember that everything you see is transient. Look up at the sky which will be destroyed and the sun which will fall. All the stars, animals, fish, everything that is beautiful and even the earth itself will die and in an instant will be nothing. This knowledge should be a consolation for you. Do not think of your grief in itself or it will appear unbearable, but consider it in relation to the wider human situation and then you will be able to find consolation for it. And in addition to these reasons you should consider your husband and offer each other mutual support.

I do not think that words alone can offer an adequate consolation and so you must pray in the present circumstances. I shall pray that God will touch your heart with his inexpressible power, illuminating your heart with the light of reason so that you may find consolation within yourself.

Also in the Spirituality
of the Fathers Series:

Born to New Life

by

Cyprian of Carthage

Cyprian of Carthage lived in troubled times. His freshness
and topicality are in part due to this, because his world,
as ours, was characterized by restlessness, insecurity and
injustice. Yet his modern tone comes also from the way
he responded to the world he lived in: he has intense twin
concerns for the mystical life and for social justice.

In one way in particular, however, he differs sharply from
the outlook of today's world. He is markedly other-worldly.
Indeed, his thinking and lifestyle are completely con-
ditioned by the awareness that everything will pass away,
and that the present life has value only in a larger perspective. Possibly it is here, as much as where he shares
contemporary attitudes, that he can teach us a great deal,
and we can learn to taste the new life he experienced if
we listen attentively to him telling of his discoveries.

Like *Gateway to Paradise* this book has been edited
by Dr Oliver Davies and translated into modern English by
Tim Witherow. It has a fascinating introduction by Cyprian
Smith OSB, which helps the anthology provide us with a
way of penetrating the very deep spirituality of Cyprian
of Carthage.

ISBN 0 904287 38 6

Day by Day with the Fathers

edited by

Thomas Spidlik

This collection of penetrating and profound sayings of the Fathers of the Church offers us a way of drinking deeply from the fountain of their wisdom. Indeed, because the book has a thought for every day, it is a powerful tool for daily, personal meditation.

Each month follows a theme, looking at issues vital for human life. The book is, therefore, a treasure-trove to be dipped into or used consistently throughout the year, and it will always provide a host of useful thoughts. But, however it is used, it constantly reveals the richness of genuine Christian spirituality.

ISBN 0 904287 39 4

Meditations

by

Chiara Lubich

Chiara Lubich's *Meditations* are fast becoming considered by many people to be spiritual classics. They have something in them for everyone.

Yet a strange quality of darkness and light characterizes them. In a sense they dazzle us. Their beauty vibrates with such a depth of meaning, that they seem almost from another world. And in a way they are. They express, very clearly, something of heaven's viewpoint. And the human and the heavenly way of seeing things rarely coincide.

Nevertheless, the appeal of the *Meditations* is hard to deny. They tug at the heart and fill the reader with a thirst for the Infinite, while at the same time pointing out quite down to earth ways of living. For these writings are nothing if not eminently practical, something that can be transformed into daily life, and indeed, when lived, they transform daily life with their own beauty.

ISBN 0 904287 29 7